BASIC OF ISLAM

Istinjaa, Wudhu, Ghusal, & Salaah

Including

SUNNATS OF
OUR BELOVED NABI MUHAMMAD

Sunnats of Eating, Drinking, Sleeping, Awakening, Wearing clothes & General Sunnats

THE EVERYDAY LIFE OF A MUSLIM
A MUST FOR ALL MAKTABS

PRACTICAL METHOD OF PERFORMING SALAAH

Prepared by:

Jamiatul Ulama (KZN) - Ta'limi Board
Isipingo Beach, 4115, South Africa
(+27) 031 912 2172 - info@talimiboardkzn.org

Published by:

Islamic Book Store

Contents

Wudhu 4

Ghusal 6

Azaan 7

Salaah 8

Sunnats 15

    Sunnats of the toilet.. 15

    Sunnats of Eating 16

    Sunnats of drinking 17

    Sunnats of Sleeping... 17

    Sunnats when Awakening....................................... 18

    Sunnats when wearing clothes 19

    Sunnats of the home... 19

    General Sunnats.. 20

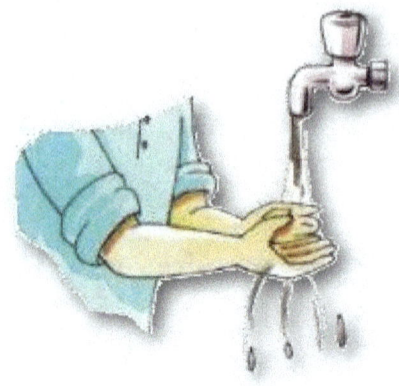

WUDHU

The following is the Sunnah method of making wudhu:

1. Make intention, recite the dua:

   "Bismillah wal hamdulillah"

   and wash both hands upto the wrists three times.

2. Clean your teeth with a miswaak and gargle your mouth three times.

3. Put water into the nostrils three times with the right hand and clean the nose with the left hand.

4. Wash your full face three times from the hairline to the chin and from one earlobe to the other.

5. Wash your right and left arms including the elbows three times and then make khilaal of your fingers.
6. Make masah of your whole head once.
7. Make masah of both your ears and your nape once.
8. Wash both your feet including the ankles and make khilaal of the toes.
9. Read the dua after wudhu.

Note: It is fardh to;
1. Wash the full face once.
2. Wash both the arms including the elbows once.
3. Mash of quarter the head once.
4. Wash both feet including the ankles once.

Teacher Tip:
Take the pupils to the wudhu khana and demonstrate the method of wudhu to them. Thereafter make each child make wudhu in front of you and correct any mistakes.

The following is the Sunnah method of making ghusal:

1. Make niyyah (intention) and wash both hands up to the wrists thrice.

2. Make istinjaa (i.e. to wash both the private parts) and wash off any najaasat (impurity) that may be on the body.

3. Perform wudhu according to the sunnah manner.

4. Pour water thrice over the head, thereafter thrice over the right shoulder and then thrice over the left shoulder in such a manner that the entire body gets wet.

Note: It is fardh (compulsory) to gargle the mouth, put water into the nose and wet the entire body.

Teacher Tip:
Bring a bucket and jug to the class.

AZAAN

The Azaan should be given in a beautiful voice in the following manner:

اَللهُ اَكْبَرُ اللهُ اَكْبَرُ ۔ اَللهُ اَكْبَرُ اللهُ اَكْبَرُ

اَشْهَدُ اَنْ لَّاۤ اِلٰهَ اِلَّا الله اَشْهَدُ اَنْ لَّاۤ اِلٰهَ اِلَّا الله

اَشْهَدُ اَنَّ مُحَمَّدًا رَّسُوْلُ اللهِ اَشْهَدُ اَنَّ مُحَمَّدًا رَّسُوْلُ اللهِ

حَيَّ عَلَى الصَّلٰوةِ حَيَّ عَلَى الصَّلٰوةِ

حَيَّ عَلَى الْفَلَاحْ حَيَّ عَلَى الْفَلَاحْ

اَللهُ اَكْبَرُ اللهُ اَكْبَرُ

لَاۤ اِلٰهَ اِلَّا اللهُ

SALAAH

PRACTICAL METHOD OF PERFORMING A TWO RAKAAT SALAAH
(FOR MALES)

- Make niyyah (intention) and face the Qiblah.

- Thereafter raise both hands up to the ears and with the palms facing the Qiblah say: *Allahu Akbar*, and fold both hands below the navel.

- Thereafter recite Sanaa:

سُبْحَانَكَ اللّٰهُمَّ وَبِحَمْدِكَ وَتَبَارَكَ اسْمُكَ وَتَعَالٰى جَدُّكَ وَلَا اِلٰهَ غَيْرُكَ

- Read Ta'awwuz:

اَعُوْذُ بِاللّٰهِ مِنَ الشَّيْطَانِ الرَّجِيْمِ

- Then recite Tasmiyah:

$$بِسْمِ اللهِ الرَّحْمٰنِ الرَّحِيْمِ$$

- Now recite Surah Faatiha (Alhamdu).

- Thereafter recite any Surah you know, and then

- while saying *Allahu Akbar* go into Ruku.

- In Ruku hold the knees with your hands and spread the fingers around the knees. Recite the Tasbeeh of Ruku three times:

$$سُبْحَانَ رَبِّيَ الْعَظِيْمِ$$

- Stand up while saying:

$$سَمِعَ اللهُ لِمَنْ حَمِدَهْ$$

- While standing in Qaumah (standing up) say:

$$رَبَّنَا لَكَ الْحَمْدُ$$

- While Saying Takbeer, go into Sajdah by first placing your knees, then both the hands, the nose and lastly the forehead between both hands on the ground.

- In Sajdah recite the Tasbeeh thrice:

$$سُبْحَانَ رَبِّيَ الْأَعْلٰى$$

- Thereafter, while saying the Takbeer, sit upright in Jalsa. One must sit on the left foot with the right foot straight up and the toes facing the Qiblah.

- Now repeat the Takbeer and go back into Sajdah in the same manner as in the first Sajdah.

- On finishing the second Sajdah, one Rakaat has been completed. After completing the second Sajdah stand up while saying *Allahu Akbar* without putting the hands on the ground.

- Now the second Rakaat will begin as in the first.

- Recite the Tasmiya, Surah Faatiha and a Surah, perform the Ruku, Qaumah and both Sajdahs. After the second Sajdah do not stand up but go into the sitting position and recite Tashahhud followed by Durood-e-Ibraaheem and the dua after Durood-e-Ibraaheem.

Tashah-hud

اَلتَّحِيَّاتُ لِلّٰهِ وَالصَّلَوٰتُ وَالطَّيِّبَاتُ اَلسَّلَامُ عَلَيْكَ اَيُّهَا النَّبِيُّ وَرَحْمَةُ اللّٰهِ وَبَرَكَاتُهُ اَلسَّلَامُ عَلَيْنَا وَعَلٰى عِبَادِ اللّٰهِ الصَّالِحِيْنَ اَشْهَدُ اَنْ لَّا اِلٰهَ اِلَّا اللّٰهُ وَاَشْهَدُ اَنَّ مُحَمَّدًا عَبْدُهُ وَرَسُوْلُهُ

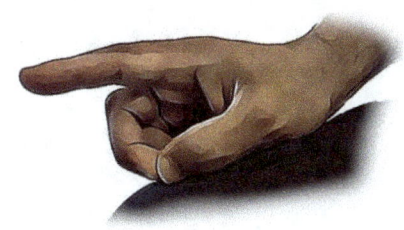

Durood-e-Ibraaheem

اَللّٰهُمَّ صَلِّ عَلٰى مُحَمَّدٍ وَّعَلٰى اٰلِ مُحَمَّدٍ كَمَا صَلَّيْتَ عَلٰى اِبْرَاهِيْمَ وَعَلٰى اٰلِ اِبْرَاهِيْمَ اِنَّكَ حَمِيْدٌ مَّجِيْدٌ

اَللّٰهُمَّ بَارِكْ عَلٰى مُحَمَّدٍ وَّعَلٰى اٰلِ مُحَمَّدٍ كَمَا بَارَكْتَ عَلٰى اِبْرَاهِيْمَ وَعَلٰى اٰلِ اِبْرَاهِيْمَ اِنَّكَ حَمِيْدٌ مَّجِيْدٌ

Dua after Durood-e-Ibraaheem

اَللّٰهُمَّ اِنِّيْ ظَلَمْتُ نَفْسِيْ ظُلْمًا كَثِيْرًا وَّلَا يَغْفِرُ الذُّنُوْبَ اِلَّا اَنْتَ فَاغْفِرْلِيْ مَغْفِرَةً مِّنْ عِنْدِكَ وَارْحَمْنِيْ اِنَّكَ اَنْتَ الْغَفُوْرُ الرَّحِيْمُ

- Lastly make the salaam:

اَلسَّلَامُ عَلَيْكُمْ وَرَحْمَةُ اللّٰهِ

- First turn the head towards the right and make salaam and then towards the left and make salaam.

Differences in the Salaah of Females

1) **Takbeer-e-Tahreema** (The first takbeer)

- Females should raise their hands up to the chest without exposing their hands. i.e. the hands should remain beneath the Burqah.
- She must not bend her head forward nor make her head touch her chest.

2) **Qiyaam** (standing posture)

- She should keep her feet together and tie her hands on her chest in such a way that the palm of her right hand is placed on the back of her left palm.
- She will not tie her hands below the navel (as men do).

3) **Ruku** (Bowing)

- She should only bow down so much that the tips of her fingers are able to touch the top of her knees.

- Her fingers and feet should be kept together.
- She should also ensure that her elbows touch her sides in Ruku.

4) **Sajdah** (Prostration)

- Her stomach and thighs must be kept together with her forearms placed flat on the ground and her feet horizontally facing towards the right.
- Her fingers should face the Qiblah in Sajdah.

5) **Qa'dah** (Sitting Posture)

- She should not sit on the left leg (as men do) but rather sit on the floor.
- Her feet should be spread out horizontally on the ground towards the right side.
- Her both hands should be kept on the upper part of the thighs with the fingers kept together.

6) Women must not raise their voices when reciting in Salaah.

Sunnats

of our Beloved Nabi Muhammad

Sunnats of the toilet

1. *Enter* the toilet with your *head covered*.
2. Enter the toilet with *shoes*.

3. Recite the *dua* before entering the toilet.
4. Enter with the *left foot*.
5. *Sit* and urinate. One should never urinate whilst standing.
6. One should *not face* or show ones back towards the *Qiblah*.
7. One should *not speak* in the toilet.
8. Be very *careful* of the *splashes* of urine. *(Being unmindful in this regard causes one to be punished in the grave.)*
9. Wash yourself with *water* using your *left hand*.
10. *Leave* the toilet with the *right foot*.
11. Recite the *dua* after coming out of the toilet.

Sunnats of Eating

1. Spread out a cloth on the floor before eating.
2. Wash both hands up to the wrists
3. Rinse the mouth.
4. Remove your shoes before eating.
5. Sit on the floor and eat.
6. Before eating recite 'Bismillah wa'ala barakatillah' aloud.
7. When eating, sit with either both knees on the ground or one knee raised or both knees raised.
8. Do not lean and eat.
9. Eat with the right hand.
10. Eat with three fingers if possible.
11. One should not eat very hot food.
12. Do not blow on the food.
13. Eat from the side that is in front of you.
14. If a morsel of food falls down, pick it up, clean it and eat it.
15. Do not find fault with the food.
16. Clean the plate and other utensils thoroughly after eating. By doing this, the utensil makes dua for one's forgiveness.
17. After eating, lick the fingers.

18. Recite the dua after eating.
19. Remove the food before getting up.
20. Wash both the hands after meals.
21. Thereafter gargle the mouth.

Sunnats of drinking

1. Recite "Bismillah" before drinking.
2. A Muslim should drink with the right hand. Shaytaan drinks with the left hand.
3. Sit and drink.
4. Do not drink directly from the jug or bottle. One should pour the contents into a glass first and then drink.
5. Drink in 3 breaths (sips), removing the utensil from the mouth after each sip.
6. After drinking say "Alhamdulillah"

Sunnats of Sleeping

1. It is sunnah to sleep immediately after Esha Salaah.
2. Before going to sleep, discuss with one's family members matters pertaining to Deen. (It is best to read from the book Fazaaile Aamaal).
3. To sleep in the state of wudhu.

4. To brush the teeth with a miswaak.
5. One should change into some other clothes before going to sleep.
6. To apply surmah in both the eyes.
7. Dust the bed thrice before retiring to bed.
8. To sleep on the right hand side.
9. To sleep with the right palm under the right cheek.
10. To keep the knees slightly bent when sleeping.
11. Refrain from sleeping on one's stomach.
12. To sleep on a bed or to sleep on the floor are both sunnah.
13. To face the Qiblah.
14. To recite Surah Mulk before sleeping.
15. To recite Aayatul Kursi.
16. To recite Surah Ikhlaas, Surah Falaq and Surah Naas before sleeping 3 times and thereafter blow onto our palms and pass over the entire body thrice.
17. Recite Tasbeeh-e-Faatimi before sleeping. (i.e. 33 times Subhan Allah 33 times Alhamdulillah and 34 times Allahu Akbar.)
18. To recite the dua before sleeping.

Sunnats when Awakening

1. To wake up for Tahajjud Salaah.
2. To rub the eyes with the palms of the hands.

3. To say "Alhamdulillah" thrice and then recite "Kalima Tayyibah" on awakening.
4. Thereafter recite the dua on awakening.
5. To cleanse the mouth with a Miswaak.

Sunnats when wearing clothes

1. When putting on any garment Rasulullah ﷺ always began with the right limb.
2. When removing any garment Rasulullah ﷺ always removed the left limb first.
3. Males must wear the pants above the ankles. Females should ensure that their lower garment covers their ankles.
4. Males should wear a 'topee' (hat) or turban. Females must wear scarves/burqahs covering their hair at all times.

5. When wearing shoes, first wear the right shoe then the left.
6. When removing your shoes, first remove the left and then the right.

Sunnats of the home

1. To recite the dua before entering the home.
2. To greet those who are in the house with "Assalaamu alaykum."

3. To announce ones arrival by coughing, greeting etc. even though it may be your own house.

General Sunnats

1. Using a miswaak is a great sunnah of Rasulullah ﷺ. One who makes miswaak when making wudhu and thereafter performs salaah will receive 70 times more reward. It will also enable one to easily recite the kalimah at the time of death.
2. To have a bath on a Friday.
3. To apply itr. (this applies to men only)
4. For men to keep a beard that is one fist in length.
5. To carry one's shoes in the left hand.
6. To make wudhu at home before going to the Masjid.
7. To enter the Masjid with the right foot.
8. To leave the Masjid with the left foot.
9. To speak softly and politely.
10. To greet all Muslims by saying "Assalaamu alaykum wa rahmatullahi wa barakaatuhu."
11. To show mercy to those who are younger than you.
12. To respect your elders.
13. To respect your parents.
14. To visit a Muslim when he/she is sick.

15. To be good towards your neighbour.

16. To meet a Muslim with a smile.

17. To care for the poor and needy.

18. To keep good relations with all your relatives.

19. To be hospitable towards your guest.

20. To exchange gifts with one another.

21. To make mashwarah (consult) with one's parents, teachers or elders before doing any work.

22. To encourage people to do good.

23. To stop them from doing evil.

24. To recite some portion of the Qur-aan Shareef daily.

25. To make dua to Allah Ta'ala for all your needs.

www.ingramcontent.com/pod-product-compliance
Lightning Source LLC
LaVergne TN
LVHW020136080526
838202LV00047B/3951